ECOCRAFTS

Creative
Costumes

ECOCRAFTS

Creative
Costumes

KINGFISHER
BOSTON

KINGFISHER

a Houghton Mifflin Company imprint
222 Berkeley Street
Boston, Massachusetts 02116
www.houghtonmifflinbooks.com

First published in 2007
10 9 8 7 6 5 4 3 2 1
1TR/0507/C&C/MAR(MAR)/128OJIEX-GREEN/C

Authors: Dawn Brend, Kirsty Neale,
Cheryl Owen, Melanie Williams

For Toucan
Editor: Theresa Bebbington
Designer: Leah Germann
Photography art direction: Jane Thomas
Photographer: Andy Crawford
Editorial director: Ellen Dupont

For Kingfisher
Senior editor: Catherine Brereton
Coordinating editors: Stephanie Pliakas
and Caitlin Doyle
Art director: Mike Davis
Senior production controller: Lindsey Scott
DTP coordinator: Catherine Hibbert
DTP operator: Claire Cessford

LIBRARY OF CONGRESS CATALOGING-IN-PUBLICATION DATA
Ecocrafts. Creative costumes/Dawn Brend...[et al.].—
1st ed.
p. cm.
Includes index.
1. Costume—Juvenile literature. 2. Recycling (Waste,
etc.)—Juvenile literature. I. Brend, Dawn.
TT633.E26 2007
646.4'78—dc22
2007004137

ISBN: 978-0-7534-5968-3
Printed in China

**The paper used for the cover and text pages is
made from 100% recycled post-consumer waste.**

Contents

Ecowise

It might be hard to decide which is more fun: making your own costumes or wearing them. By creating your own costumes, you make sure that they will be special to you—no one else will have costumes that are exactly the same as yours.

As well as being really special, all of the projects in this book help the environment by using everyday objects found in your home. A lot of them are items that you would have thrown away. You'll find ways to use cardboard and newspaper to make a monster mask, use coat hangers to create wings for a fairy, turn plastic bags into a wizard's cape, and even reuse a big T-shirt to make a witch's dress. Recycling helps the planet because it reuses things that would have ended up in the trash.

Around the world, tons of garbage end up in landfills each year. In fact, in 1999 the Fresh

3 "R"s to recycling

Around half of our garbage can be recycled. Follow these steps to help prevent garbage from being sent to landfills or incinerators.

REDUCE—Encourage your parents to buy products that have little or no packaging.

REUSE—Find new ways to use jars, cans, plastic containers, and other durable items.

RECYCLE—If you can't reuse something but it can be recycled, help your parents recycle it.

6

Kills landfill in Staten Island, New York, became the largest human-made structure in the world, overtaking the Great Wall of China. Each year we create more garbage than the year before, and if we continue to do this, it's thought that we'll double the amount of garbage that we produce by 2020.

When we throw away so much garbage, we are also throwing away valuable resources. If we recycle our garbage, fewer materials will need to be mined, quarried, or grown, and less energy is used to transport these materials around the world. Another concern is that the landfills where garbage is buried are filling up—and there's not much space left to make new landfills.

What you can do

Grown out of your clothes? If they are in good condition, give them to your younger brother or sister or donate old clothes to a thrift store, which can sell them to someone who they will fit.

If your old clothes are too stained or are ripped, use the good pieces of fabric to make something else. You can even sew pieces together to make a small blanket for your favorite doll.

If you've been given old clothes, see what's in fashion in the stores and think about how you can change them. Maybe sew on some buttons in a pattern.

If a room is being redecorated, ask if you can save any old curtains, tablecloths, or even cushion covers to reuse the fabric to make something else.

Before starting a project, make sure that you have everything you need. You may have to trace a picture or do some sewing. If you're not sure how to do these things, follow the steps here. Some craft supplies are not supposed to be used by children under 13. If you're not sure if something is safe for you to use, ask an adult if it's okay. When using craft supplies that have a strong odor, work in a room that has plenty of fresh air. If an object is difficult to cut, ask an adult to help.

BASIC CRAFT KIT

Assemble a basic craft kit, which will be useful for many of these projects. And don't forget to work in an area where you don't have to worry about making a mess.

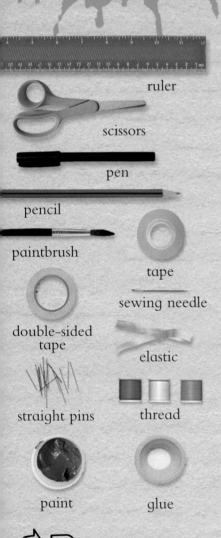

ruler

scissors

pen

pencil

paintbrush

tape

sewing needle

double-sided tape

elastic

straight pins

thread

paint

glue

Sewing Tips

Be careful when you handle sewing needles and straight pins, which are sharp and can prick you.

To thread a needle, cut the end of the thread at an angle and wet it with saliva. It will be easier to fit it through the eye of the needle.

To make a knot at the end of the thread, wrap it around your forefinger a few times, roll it off between your finger and thumb, and pull it tight.

For a finishing knot, make a tiny stitch into the fabric, wrap the thread around the needle, and pull the needle. Cut off the extra thread.

MAKING A SQUARE KNOT

You can use this knot to tie the ends of some elastic together. Once you tie the knot, trim off the ends.

STEP 1

Make a simple overhand knot by bringing the ends together and feeding the left end over the right end.

STEP 2

Make another overhand knot in the opposite direction, with the right end over the left end.

8

TYPES OF STITCHES

When making stitches, keep the spaces and stitch sizes as even as you can. The running stitch is a simple stitch to hold two seams together. If you want a really strong seam, you can use the backstitch in Steps 1 and 2 for all the stitches. To gather material, skip Steps 1 and 2 and let the knot in the thread hold it in place. Then make tacking stitches—these are simply large running stitches, but they are around 1 in. (2–3cm) long.

STEP 1

Make a backstitch by inserting the needle up through the fabric and then down behind where the thread exits the fabric, 0.2 in. (5mm) behind it.

STEP 2

Now bring the needle up again, 0.2 in. (5mm) in front of the thread. This secures the end of the thread. Now make the running stitches in Step 3.

STEP 3

Pass the needle over and under the fabric, along the seam, making a few stitches at a time and then pulling the thread. At the end make a finishing knot (see Sewing Tips, left).

TRACING A PICTURE

If you have a pencil, pen, tracing paper, and tape, you can copy any picture you want. The pencil should have soft lead (No. 2)—this will make it easier to do the rubbing over the back. Use a pen with a hard point to make the lines really crisp.

STEP 1

Tape down a sheet of tracing paper over the picture that you want to draw. Using a pen with a hard point, copy the picture onto the tracing paper.

STEP 2

Remove the tracing paper from the picture. Rub a soft-lead pencil on the back of the tracing paper so that you can see the lines that you have drawn.

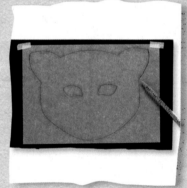

STEP 3

Tape the tracing paper where you want the picture, with the pencil side facing down. Draw over the lines with a pen. Remove the paper.

Scales and a tail

Pastel-colored plastic bags will make fantastic scales for an amazing mermaid costume. Decorate an old top and make your own special headband, and your mermaid outfit will make you a real queen of the sea!

YOU WILL NEED:

white garbage bag, ruler, scissors, double-sided tape, elastic, colored plastic bags, cardboard, pencil, old top, glue, paintbrush, paint, wrapping paper, ribbon, glitter

STEP 1

To make the skirt, cut a white garbage bag so that it is long enough to reach your ankles and is 8 in. (20cm) wider than your waist. Cut a curved shape at the bottom.

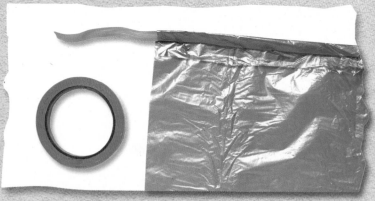

STEP 2

Place a strip of double-sided tape 1 in. (3cm) from the top of the skirt. Cut a piece of elastic a little longer than your waist. Lay it above the tape, fold over the edge of the skirt, and press it into the tape—don't let the elastic disappear into the seam. Tie the elastic ends in a knot.

STEP 3

To attach the two front edges of the skirt together, lay the skirt flat on the ground, with the opening on top. Lift up one side of the skirt and stick double-sided tape down the straight edge of the other side (stop before it curves). Push the first side down on the tape.

STEP 4

Choose plastic bags in different colors, such as pink and blue, and cut scale shapes from them. Also cut some strips of plastic, around 4–6 in. (10–15cm) long, from extra pieces of the white garbage bag.

STEP 5

Decorate the skirt by sticking the scales and strips to it. First tape the strips around the bottom of the skirt. Then, beginning at the bottom, tape a row of scales around the skirt.

STEP 6

Continue sticking the scales onto the skirt, making sure that each new row of scales overlaps the row of scales below it. Once you've finished taping on the scales, choose a few scales and glue some glitter onto them.

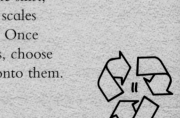

Scales and a tail

STEP 7

For the top, cut out a pair of scallop-shaped shells from a blue plastic bag.

STEP 8

Brush glue in the lines on the shells. Sprinkle glitter over the glue and let the glue dry.

STEP 9

Splatter some paint on an old, light-colored top, or ask an adult to spray some paint on it.

STEP 10

Using double-sided tape, attach the shells to the top in a bikinilike style.

STEP 11

For the headband, cut a piece of cardboard so that it fits halfway around your head and is 1.5 in. (4cm) wide. Cut some wrapping paper large enough to cover the band.

STEP 12

Brush some glue onto the cardboard and wrap the paper around it—make sure that the paper lies flat and smooth. Let the glue dry. For a neat look, cut a curved shape at each end.

STEP 13

Cut a piece of elastic a few inches longer than the headband. Poke a hole in each end of the band. Feed one end of the elastic into each hole and tie a knot.

STEP 14

Cut some long strips of wrapping paper and ribbon. Beginning at one end, where the cardboard meets the elastic, tape alternating lengths of ribbon and wrapping paper.

STEP 15

Continue taping the strips around the band until you reach the other end of the elastic. Finally, curl the strips by running a ruler or scissors sharply along them (if you use scissors, you should ask an adult for help).

Wear the headband with the strips in front and pretend that they are mermaid hair.

Make a really big splash when you put on this great mermaid outfit!

A fairy-tale fairy

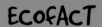

You can turn an old tank top and lacy tablecloth or curtains into a beautiful fairy dress. Add your own special wings and a wand, and you'll soon have a magical costume. A pink top and pink plastic bags will make the best outfit. Be careful when handling the pins.

YOU WILL NEED:

old tank top, pen, ruler or tape measure, scissors, lace tablecloth or curtains, straight pins, thread, sewing needle, fake jewels, glue, paintbrush, two metal clothes hangers, tape, plastic bags, elastic, cardboard, wooden plant stake, paint, ribbon, sequins

STEP 1

To make the dress, put on your tank top and mark with a pen where it sits at your waist. Take it off and at the mark draw a line around the top.

STEP 2

To make the skirt section of the dress, cut the lace tablecloth or cutains into four rectanglar panels, each one around 20 x 27 in. (50 x 70cm).

14

STEP 3

For each panel, fold it over diagonally so that two corners form triangles at the bottom (as shown here). The middle section of the fold will be attached to the dress.

STEP 4

Make pleats along the middle section of the fold by overlapping the fabric every 1 in. (2–3cm) and holding each pleat in place with a straight pin.

A floral pattern makes pretty lacy panels, but you can use any pattern that you want.

STEP 5

Pin one panel to the front of the top (along the line at the waist), one to the back, and one to each side. Sew them on using a running stitch (see page 9), passing the needle through all of the layers of fabric. Or ask an adult to sew them on for you. Remove the pins.

STEP 6

Decorate the top by adding fake jewels or sequins onto it, making a border along the top and a heart in the center. You can use self-stick fake jewels or glue them in place. If you want, you can also glue on some flower decorations.

A fairy-tale fairy

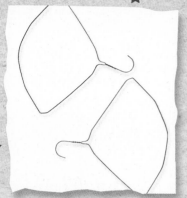

STEP 7

For the wings, bend out the bottom of two metal clothes hangers so that they form a winglike shape.

STEP 8

Ask an adult to twist the two hooked ends together. Wrap tape around the hooks to secure them.

STEP 9

Place a plastic bag over a hanger, wrap the top end around the hook section, and tape it in place.

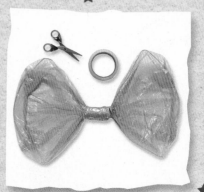

STEP 10

Repeat for the second wing, wrapping the end neatly around the hook section for a nice finish.

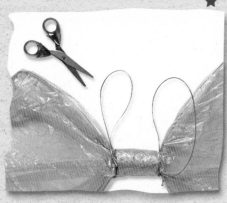

STEP 11

Cut two pieces of elastic long enough to loop around your arms. Tape them to the wings.

STEP 12

For the wand, draw a star on some cardboard (a cereal box is ideal) and cut it out. Use the star as a template to make a second star in exactly the same size.

STEP 13

Ask an adult to cut a wooden plant stake so that it is 18 in. (45cm) long. Paint the stars and the stake. Leave them to dry.

STEP 14

Wind some ribbon around the stake and tape down the ends. Tape a star to the top of the stake and then tape thin pieces of ribbon to the back of the star.

STEP 15

Glue the second star to the back of the first star and decorate it by gluing on some sequins.

You'll feel like a real fairy wearing these wings and dress. To make them extra special, glue some sequins to the skirt and add glitter to the wings.

Princess for a day

The cape and tiara will make this princess dress a dream come true. Making this outfit is a great way to reuse old fabrics. When choosing the fabric for the skirt, make sure that there is enough for the sleeves, too.

YOU WILL NEED:

fabric for the skirt and sleeves, scissors, sewing needle, thread, short-sleeved top, straight pins, glue, fake jewels, sequins, tape measure or ruler, lace or sheer curtain, two safety pins, elastic, heavy fabric, curtain tie rope, trimming (from an old curtain or cushion), cardboard, silver paint, paintbrush, headband, tape chalk, pink fabric

STEP 1

For the sleeves, cut two semicircles from the fabric for the skirt. Make tacking stitches (see page 9) along the straight edge of each sleeve.

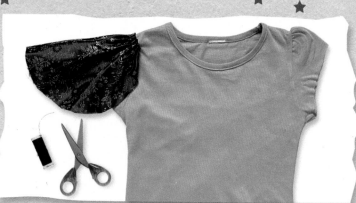

STEP 2

For each sleeve, pull the thread to gather the fabric, making sure that it fits on the short-sleeved top. Use straight pins to hold the sleeve in place at the top. Sew the sleeve to the top using a running stitch (see page 9).

STEP 3

Dab some glue onto the back of some sequins and fake jewels and stick them around the neckline on the top. Choose your favorite jewel to use in the middle of the neckline.

STEP 4

Cut a piece of fabric long enough for a knee-length skirt and 12 in. (30cm) wider than your waist. Cut a lace or sheer curtain the same width, but reaching your ankles.

Pin an end of the elastic to the fabric so that it doesn't slip into the hem as you work.

STEP 5

Fold over the top 2 in. (5cm) of the curtain and sew along it to make a hem. Attach a safety pin to one end of a piece of elastic that is 4 in. (10cm) longer than your waist. Push the pin through the hem to feed the elastic through it. Tie the ends in a knot. Repeat for the skirt.

STEP 6

For the cape, cut a piece of fabric that is big enough to drape over your shoulders and to reach below your knees. Sew a hem in the top as in Step 5, but feed a curtain tie rope through it. Glue some trimming to the bottom. Leave to dry.

Princess for a day

STEP 7

For the tiara, use a headband to trace the bottom edge onto a piece of cardboard, draw a tab, and then draw the top curvy edge, as shown here. Cut out the tiara shape.

STEP 8

Paint the tiara silver on one side. Once it is dry, paint the other side of the tiara. Leave it to dry.

STEP 9

Fit the tiara around the headband and fold over the tab. Tape the tab firmly onto the headband.

STEP 10

Choose some sequins and fake jewels that match those used on the dress, dab some glue on the back, and use them to decorate the tiara. Leave the tiara to dry.

When you're ready to be a princess for a day, put on your dress, tie the sash around it, and make a pretty bow in the back. Now you're ready for your cape and tiara.

STEP 11

For the sash, fold a piece of fabric 8 x 43 in. (20 x 110cm) in half lengthwise, with the sides that you want to see pressed together. Sew the long edge with a running stitch (see page 9). Turn it inside out and sew the short ends together.

STEP 12

For a flower, fold a piece of fabric 4 x 8 in. (10 x 20cm) in half lengthwise, with the sides that you don't want to see pressed together. Sew the long edge with a tacking stitch (see page 9). Gather the fabric into a circle. Sew the short ends together.

STEP 13

Glue a fake jewel to the middle of the flower and leave it to dry. Once it is dry, sew the flower to the center of the sash.

Wicked witch

All witches need a pointy hat, and this one is very special. Wear it with the wicked witch's dress, made from an old black T-shirt (man's size).

YOU WILL NEED:

cardboard, ruler, pencil, scissors, tape, glue, black paint, paintbrush, tape measure, yarn, star-shaped stickers, dress, large black T-shirt, chalk, paper or newspaper, straight pins, sewing needle, thread

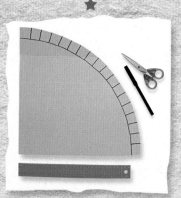

STEP 1

For a hat, draw a quarter circle onto a piece of cardboard, with the straight sides 15 in. (38cm) long. Cut out the hat and then cut slits at the curved edge.

STEP 2

For the brim, draw a circle with a 14 in. (35cm) diameter (the distance across the middle) onto cardboard. Draw an oval shape in the center that will fit your head. Cut out the circles.

STEP 3

Roll up the quarter circle into a cone shape and tape the edges together. Bend out the slits cut into the end of the cone and glue the brim to the slits. Paint the hat black. Leave it to dry.

STEP 4

To make witch's hair, cut some pieces of yarn and glue them inside the back of the hat. Stick some star-shaped stickers around the hat.

22

STEP 5

Trace around a dress that fits you onto paper or newspaper and cut out the shape. Use straight pins to pin the paper dress to a large black T-shirt turned inside out—make sure that the necklines match up.

STEP 6

Trace around the paper dress with a piece of chalk. Remove the straight pins and the paper dress. Cut out the shape of the dress. (You might want to use straight pins to hold the seams together.)

STEP 7

Using a running stitch (see page 9), sew along the seams up the sides of the dress and under the arms.

STEP 8

Turn the dress right side out. Using scissors, cut a jagged fringe along the bottom edge.

Even wicked witches can have fun, so try wearing this outfit with some bright, striped tights, a nose from a costume store, and go for a ride on a witch's broomstick!

Purr-fect black cat

With some cardboard, socks, and a few other items, you'll soon be going on the prowl as the "top cat" in your house. Our cat is black, but you can choose any color you want.

YOU WILL NEED:
●●●
black and white cardboard, scissors, black marker, glue, paintbrush, pink button, elastic, pink felt, three pairs of black knee socks, 1-inch-wide black elastic

STEP 1
To trace a mask from black cardboard (see page 9) and a muzzle from white cardboard, use the templates on page 46. Cut them out.

STEP 2
Draw the mouth and whiskers on the muzzle with a black marker.

STEP 3
Spread some glue on the back of the muzzle. Glue the muzzle on the mask.

STEP 4
For the nose, stick a pink button to the muzzle with glue. Allow the glue to dry.

STEP 5

Ask an adult to poke a hole in each side of the mask. Thread elastic through the holes and make knots in the ends.

STEP 6

Cut four sets of paw pads from pink felt. Attach each set to the toe end of a black sock with glue.

STEP 7

For the tail, turn a sock inside out and sew along the center (or ask an adult to sew the sock). Turn the tail right side out.

STEP 8

Tie some elastic around your waist and knot the ends together. Cut off the extra elastic. Take off the elastic and sew the top of the sock at the knot.

You can paint cardboard from a cereal box to get the right colors!

For the complete look, slip the tail around your waist, put the socks over your hands and feet, and put on the mask. Now all you need to do is practice your meows!

25

A wise wizard

For the best-looking wizard, collect plastic bags that are black, silver, and gold. Along with some cardboard from a cereal box and a few other items, these bags can be turned into a great wizard costume.

YOU WILL NEED:

plastic bags, scissors, double-sided tape, string, ruler, cardboard, pencil, paint, paintbrush, glitter, glue, elastic, white tissue paper

ECOFACT

Plastic bags and garbage bags are made from low-density polyethylene, a thin type of plastic that is not recycled. Between 7 and 12 million plastic bags are used in England and Wales each year. Around 120,000 plastic bags make up one ton of plastic.

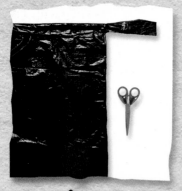

STEP 1

To make the cape, cut out a rectangle from a black plastic bag that's big enough to use as a cape. Cut a strip to use as a tie.

STEP 2

Place a strip of double-sided tape 1 in. (3cm) from the top of the cape. Lay the plastic strip above it and then fold over the top edge of the cape, pressing it into the tape.

STEP 3

Make cuts around every 2 in. (5cm) up the length of the cape, stopping a little before you reach the top. Try to keep the cuts straight and even.

STEP 4

Choose plastic bags in wizardy colors such as silver and gold. Cut them into strips that are 2 in. (5cm) wide. Tape the strips to the inside of your cape along the top edge.

26

STEP 5

To make a hat, draw a cone shape onto a large piece of cardboard. First use some string to measure around your head. The distance between the two corners at the bottom of the cone should be a few inches longer than the length of the string. Cut out the shape.

STEP 6

Stick double-sided tape along a straight edge, roll up the hat, and press the other edge into the tape. Paint the hat black. When it is dry, add glitter to the rim and paint on some stars.

STEP 7

To make a beard, draw a pair of lips onto cardboard and cut them out. Poke a hole in each end with a pencil. Cut a piece of elastic that will fit around your head, insert each end into a hole, and tie a square knot.

STEP 8

Rip some white tissue paper into three beard shapes, each one slighter larger than the previous one. Layer them, with the largest on the bottom and the smallest on the top, and glue them together. Glue on the mouth. When it is dry, cut out a mouth opening.

Put on your beard, cape, and hat to become a spellbinding wizard. If you want a wand to cast spells, follow the instructions on pages 16 and 17, but ask a grownup to spray-paint it silver instead of using the fairy design shown there.

Monster party

By using some cardboard, layers of newspaper, and other items often found around your house, you can make these monstrous hands and face.

YOU WILL NEED:

strong cardboard, pencil, scissors, thin cardboard, black marker, glue, kitchen sponge, ruler, drinking straw, tape, newspaper or an old telephone book, wallpaper paste, string, green paint, paintbrush, four bolts, yarn, thin elastic, dowel stick or wooden plant stake, green sweater or sweatshirt

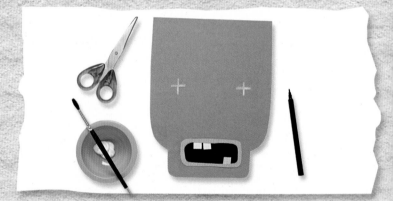

STEP 1

Copy the shape of the mask shown above onto a piece of cardboard that is 8 in. (20cm) high and 6 in. (16cm) wide. Make crosses for the eyes. Cut out the mask and then cut out the eyes.

STEP 2

Cut a pair of squarish lips from thin cardboard. Place them on the mask, trace around them, and remove the lips. Color the area inside the line with a black marker. Cut three teeth from white cardboard. Glue the top of each tooth behind the lips. Glue the lips to the front of the mask.

28

STEP 3

Cut a triangular piece of kitchen sponge to make a nose and glue it to the mask. Cut a 7-in. (18-cm) piece of a drinking straw and stick it down behind the mask as above, using a piece of newspaper and wallpaper paste.

STEP 4

Cover the mask and the straw ends in newspaper and wallpaper paste. Cut a 4-in. (10-cm) long piece of string and six other pieces of string that are 1 in. (3cm) long. While the paper is wet, stick down the string on the forehead to create a gruesome scar.

STEP 5

Paint the mask bright green. You might need to use a few coats of paint. Leave each coat to dry before painting the next one.

STEP 6

Slide two bolts along each painted straw end. Add a blob of glue to hold them in place.

STEP 7

Cut two 0.5 x 2 in. (1 x 4.5cm) strips of black cardboard to make eyebrows and a 2 x 6 in. (6 x 17cm) piece to make hair. Put glue onto one side of each piece and then press short pieces of black yarn onto it. Once it is dry, cut the yarn straight across.

Monster party

STEP 8

Glue the eyebrows onto the monster face and glue the hair behind the mask. Poke two holes on each side of the mask, using scissors. Feed the ends of a piece of elastic through each hole and tie knots at the ends.

STEP 9

To make monster hands, trace around a grownup's hands onto cardboard and cut out the shapes.

STEP 10

Tape a dowel stick or wooden plant stake securely to the back of one cardboard hand.

STEP 11

Scrunch newspaper into balls. Glue the balls over the back of the other hand.

STEP 12

Place the two hands together so that the scrunched-up paper and stick are sandwiched inside. Tape them together around the edges.

STEP 13

Tear more newspaper into small pieces and use wallpaper paste to stick them to the hand. Cover with a layer of newspaper.

STEP 14

Repeat Steps 9 to 13 for the second hand. Cut ten fingernails from a kitchen sponge. Glue them to the end of each finger.

30

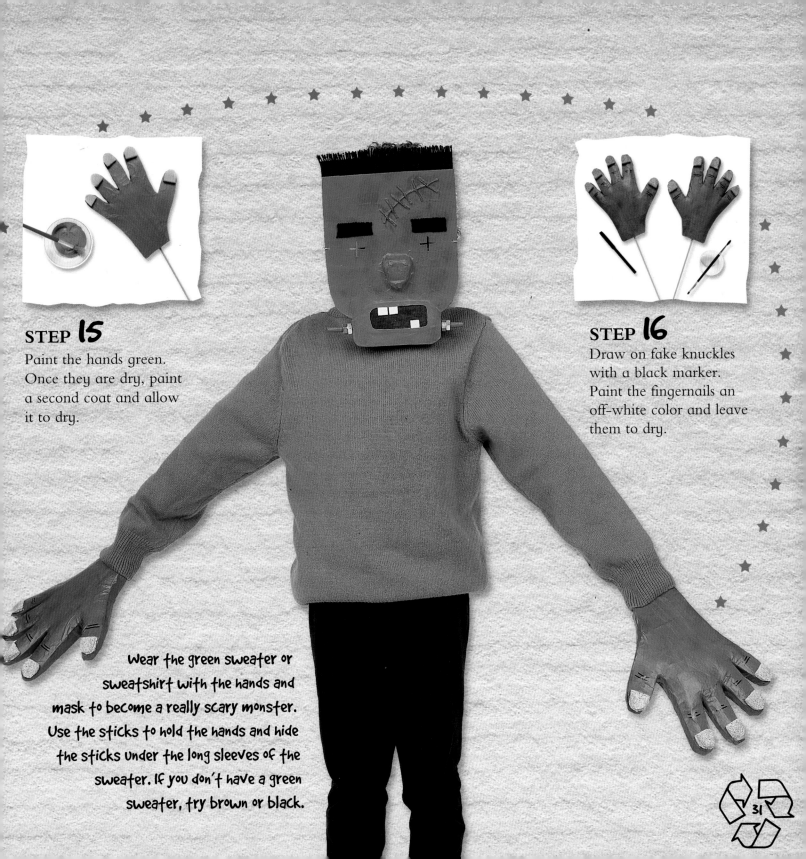

STEP 15

Paint the hands green. Once they are dry, paint a second coat and allow it to dry.

STEP 16

Draw on fake knuckles with a black marker. Paint the fingernails an off-white color and leave them to dry.

Wear the green sweater or sweatshirt with the hands and mask to become a really scary monster. Use the sticks to hold the hands and hide the sticks under the long sleeves of the sweater. If you don't have a green sweater, try brown or black.

Skull and bones

With a pair of socks and gloves, some cardboard, and a garbage bag, you can become a really frightening skeleton. Use the biggest and thickest bag that you can find to make the best skeleton.

YOU WILL NEED:
....
chalk, black garbage bag, scissors, double-sided tape, white paint, paintbrush, old pair of gloves, old pair of socks, cardboard, pen, pencil, elastic

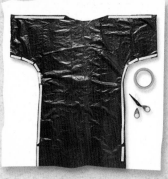

STEP 1
With chalk, draw a T-shirt shape (and neckline) onto a black garbage bag. Cut it out. Use double-sided tape to tape the edges together.

STEP 2
Cut an opening down the back. Start to paint a skeleton on the front by painting the spine down the middle. Add ribs and the shoulder and arm bones to it.

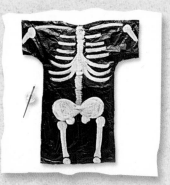

STEP 3
Continue painting the skeleton, adding the pelvis (hipbones) and leg bones. Leave it to dry and then paint bones on the back side of the bag.

STEP 4
On a pair of old gloves, paint the wrist bones at the bottom and then paint the small bones of the fingers. Let the paint dry.

STEP 5

Cut a piece of cardboard around the size of your foot and slide it inside of an old sock. This will flatten the sock to make it easier to paint.

STEP 6

For each sock, paint the anklebones, then the bones for each toe, and finish with the leg bones. Allow the paint to dry. (Don't forget to remove the cardboard.)

No one will ever guess who is hiding inside of this scary skeleton costume.

STEP 7

Draw a 6 x 10 in. (16 x 25cm) skull on cardboard, with eyes, nose, and teeth as shown. Cut out the mask and eyes. Cut around the teeth and nose, leaving them attached.

STEP 8

Paint the skull white. Once it is dry, paint black around the mouth, nose, and eyes. Poke holes in each side, using a pencil. Feed the ends of a piece of elastic through the holes and tie them.

33

Feisty fire breather

A fire-breathing dragon will be a real match in a battle against a shining knight (see pages 40–43). You can make your costume from some plastic bags, cereal boxes, and a plastic soda bottle.

YOU WILL NEED:
● ●

cardboard, pen, scissors, paint, paintbrush, plastic soda bottle, glue, elastic, paper, green garbage bag, tape, ribbon

ECOFACT
The number of plastic bottles recycled in the U.K. since 2002 has doubled, and 727 million plastic bottles were recycled in 2004. But this is only 7.9 percent of plastic bottles used in homes. Around 9.2 billion plastic bottles are thrown away each year.

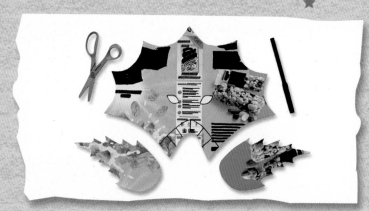

STEP 1
For the mask, using the template on page 47, trace the face and ears onto a piece of cardboard (see page 9). Cut out the face and ears and make sure that you also cut out the eyes.

STEP 2
Paint the face and ears bright green. When the paint is dry, cut slits in the bottom of the mask to make flaps (these are marked on the template).

STEP 3

Ask a grownup to cut the end off a large plastic soda bottle. Then ask the grownup to make a pair of holes for the nostrils (the flames will fit into these), as well as a slit to fit the tongue in.

STEP 4

Paint the bottle green to match the mask and leave it to dry. Paint in the white teeth and outline the teeth with gold paint. Add a decorative gold edge around the mouth and black around the nostrils.

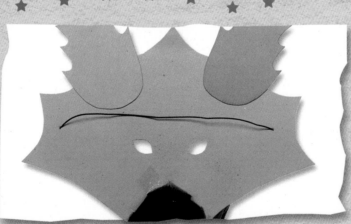

STEP 5

When the paint is dry, glue the ears to the top of the mask, sticking them onto the back of the mask. Let the glue dry.

STEP 6

Poke a hole in each side of the mask. Cut a piece of elastic that will fit around your head when it is attached to the mask. Feed one end into a hole and make a knot at the end. Feed the other end into the second hole, test the fit, and tie a knot. Cut off the extra elastic.

STEP 7

Place the bottle over the bottom of the mask and fold the tabs into it. Glue the tabs to the bottle and leave it to dry.

Feisty fire breather

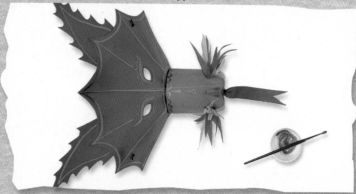

STEP 8

Cut pieces of yellow and red paper to make flames and also cut a piece of red paper to make a forked tongue. Glue these into the slits in the bottle. Finish the mask by painting some decorative lines using gold paint.

STEP 9

For the wings, cut open a large green plastic bag, cutting down one side and along the bottom. Unfold the bag that so you can find the top edge of the wings—use a long edge of the rectangle as the top.

STEP 10

Fold the bag in half from side to side and then draw a border of triangular shapes with a pen along two unfolded edges. Cut out the border. Unfold the bag.

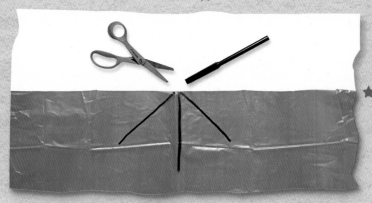

STEP 11

Make a neck opening in the middle of the straight top edge by drawing three lines 4 in. (10cm) long, with the middle one straight down and the two outer ones at 45 degree angles, as shown. Cut slits along the lines. Paint on scales and lines with gold paint. Leave it to dry.

36

STEP 12

Cut a piece of ribbon that is long enough to fit around your neck and tie a bow. Place it centered at the neck opening, fold the tabs over it, and glue them down.

STEP 13

Cut some elastic to fit around your wrist and fold it in a loop. Tape it to the top point on one side of the wings. Repeat for the other side.

To wear your wings, tie the ribbon around your neck and slide your wrists through the loops. When your mask is hiding your face, who wouldn't be scared of such a ferocious fire-breathing dragon?

A shining knight

You can make your very own sword, tabard, shield, and helmet to become a knight in shining armor. You'll be ready to fight off dragons as you rescue damsels in distress.

YOU WILL NEED:
....
felt (use two different colors), ruler, scissors, black pen, pair of compasses, glue, corrugated cardboard, paint, paintbrush, paper, pencil, aluminum foil, two brass fasteners, elastic

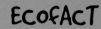

STEP 1

To make the tabard, fold a piece of 16 x 60 in. (150 x 40cm) felt in half, with the short edges together. For the neck opening, draw a 7-in. (19-cm) diameter semicircle on the fold and cut it out.

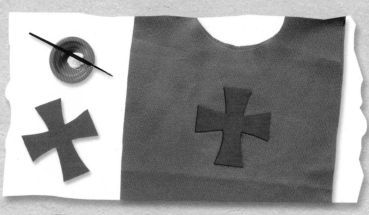

STEP 2

Follow the design shown here to draw a 6-in. (16-cm) cross onto a piece of red felt—make the bottom part of the cross a little longer than the side and top parts. Cut out the cross. Glue the cross to the front of the tabard.

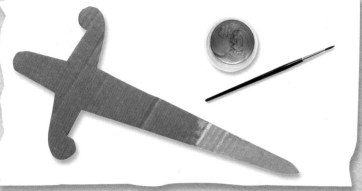

STEP 3

Draw a 16-in. (40-cm) long sword shape, as shown here, onto paper and cut it out. Draw two swords onto corrugated cardboard, using the paper sword as a guide. Ask an adult to help you cut out the two swords. Glue the swords together and leave to dry.

STEP 4

Paint one side of the sword silver. Leave it to dry and then paint the other side silver too. (If you want, you can paint the handle a different color.)

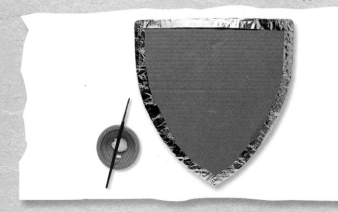

STEP 5

Draw the shape of the 13 x 15 in. (33 x 38cm) shield shown here onto corrugated cardboard. Ask an adult to cut it out. Cut a shield from aluminum foil that is the same size as the cardboard, but add 1 in. (2.5cm) to the edges. Place the cardboard shield onto the foil. Fold over the edges of the foil and glue them to the cardboard.

STEP 6

Cut another shield from foil that is the same size as the cardboard shield, but trim around 0.5 in. (5mm) from the edges. Glue the foil to the back of the cardboard shield.

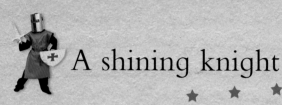

A shining knight

STEP 7

Cut out a second cross from red felt (see Step 2). Glue the cross to the front of the shield. Let the glue dry.

STEP 8

For a handle, ask an adult to cut a 1.5 x 8 in. (4 x 20cm) strip of corrugated cardboard, cutting the short edges parallel with the lines of the cardboard. Bend the handle between your fingers in order to curve it.

STEP 9

Ask an adult to poke a pair of holes in the shield and handle. Insert a brass fastener through the holes on the shield and then the holes on the handle. Open the prongs to press the handle in place.

STEP 10

Cut a visor from cardboard, making it a 8 x 17 in. (21 x 44cm) rectangle. With a long side at the top, cut out the eyeholes around 3 in. (7cm) from the top and 1.5 in. (4cm) apart. Paint the visor silver. Leave it to dry.

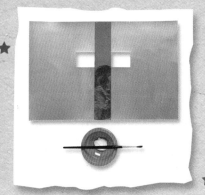

STEP 11

Cut a 1.5 x 9 in. (4 x 22cm) strip of foil. Glue the strip to the visor, folding the ends over to the back side of the visor.

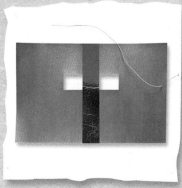

STEP 12

Ask an adult to poke a hole in each side of the visor. Feed elastic through the holes and make knots at the ends.

Put on your tabard and helmet and grab your shield and sword to turn yourself into a brave knight.

41

Shiver me timbers!

Everything a pirate needs is included in this costume: a striped shirt, bandanna, cutlass, pirate's hat, eye patch, and even a telescope. All you'll need is a parrot!

YOU WILL NEED:

old white (or light-colored) T-shirt, scissors, paint, paintbrush, red fabric, ruler or tape measure, paper, pencil, cardboard, pen, glue, tape, elastic, cardboard tubes

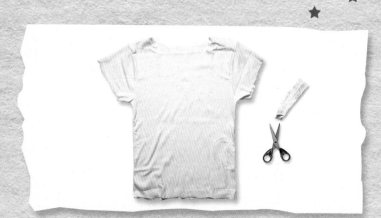

STEP 1

To make your shirt look really rugged, cut off the ends of the sleeves, the bottom of the shirt, and the neckline.

STEP 2

Paint blue stripes across the shirt and around the sleeves. Let the paint dry and then paint stripes across the back of the shirt too.

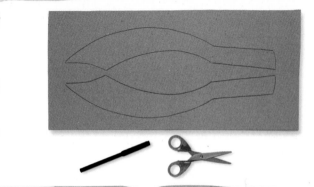

STEP 3

To make a bandanna, cut a piece of red fabric into an 18-in. (45-cm) square. Fold the square into a triangular shape.

STEP 4

Draw a cutlass shape, as shown above, onto paper, with the blade 18 in. (45cm) long and the handle 6 in. (15cm) long. Cut it out and use it to draw two cutlass shapes onto cardboard, facing opposite directions. Cut them out and glue them together.

STEP 5

Cut an oval from a piece of cardboard to make a hand protector. Make a slit in it to slip it over the cutlass handle and glue it in place.

STEP 6

Now use the paper cutlass to draw and make two more cardboard handle shapes. Cut these out and glue one to each side of the handle.

STEP 7

Paint one side of the blade silver and one side of the handle black. Once they are dry, paint the other sides.

43

Shiver me timbers!

STEP 8

Draw a pirate's hat shape onto a piece of paper and cut it out. (Measure your head beforehand to get an idea of how large to make it.) Use this to trace two pirate hat shapes onto cardboard and then cut them out.

STEP 9

Stick pieces of tape along the top edge of the two hat shapes to hold them together.

STEP 10

Paint the hat black. Once it is dry, paint a white skull and crossbones on the front of the hat.

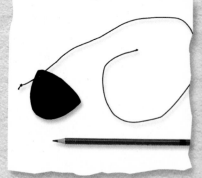

STEP 11

Cut a band of cardboard to fit your head. Tape the ends together and then tape it inside the hat.

STEP 12

Draw the shape of an eye patch onto a piece of cardboard, as shown here. Cut it out.

STEP 13

Paint the eye patch black and leave it to dry. (Don't paint the side that will be facing your eye.)

STEP 14

Poke two holes into the eye patch, using a pencil. Feed the ends of a piece of elastic through the holes and knot the ends.

STEP 15

To make a telescope, cut a slit partway down one end of a long cardboard tube. Cut a shorter piece from another tube.

STEP 16

Paint the tubes black with a silver band. Once they are dry, slip the short tube over the long tube over the slit (don't paint this end silver).

When you want to be a treasure-hunting pirate, put on your shirt, tie the bandanna around your neck, and use a wide belt to hold either your cutlass or your telescope.

45

Cat template
(for pages 24–25)

This template has been reduced to half the size so that it will fit on this page. You'll need to enlarge it by 200% on a photocopier that has 11 x 17 in. paper. Trace along the dotted line separately to make the muzzle of the cat.

Dragon template
(for pages 34–37)

This template has been reduced to half the size so that it will fit on this page. You'll need to enlarge it by 200% on a photocopier that has 11 x 17 in. paper.

Index

Special thanks to our models:
Jessica, Joseph, Oliver,
Pia, and Safia (and thanks
to their moms and dads, too).